LIVERPOOL
The Great City

HALSGROVE

First published in Great Britain in 2009
Revised and updated edition published in 2012

British Library Cataloguing-in-Publication Data
A CIP record for this title is available from the British Library

ISBN 978 0 85704 158 6

HALSGROVE
Halsgrove House,
Ryelands Business Park,
Bagley Road, Wellington, Somerset TA21 9PZ
Tel: 01823 653777   Fax: 01823 216796
email: sales@halsgrove.com

Part of the Halsgrove group of companies.
Information on all Halsgrove titles is available at: www.halsgrove.com

Printed in China by Everbest Printing Co Ltd

FOREWORD
by Ken Dodd OBE

Paul McMullin is a brilliant observer of "beauty and form…" Hmn?
This photographer obviously loves architecture and it shows – in his pictures.
In his 35 years as a lens man, this born and bred Liverpudlian started out some
time after Box Brownies were invented. Paul waited eagerly till the pics came
back from the local chemist.

Now, with new technology and digital equipment everywhere, the art of
taking photographs has changed, but not the subject matter. Over the years
he has portrayed an ever-changing Liverpool. New developments springing
up alongside the old . He has captured the city waking up and going to sleep
and all within his work – proudly depicting where the past meets the present.
Paul has studied iconic landmarks such as Lime Street – old and new. The
magnificent waterfront and the brand new shopping area 'inspiringly' called
Liverpool One.

He has captured statues standing alone in the mist with those two loyal Liver
Birds looking down protectively. Paul enjoys getting cold – standing in all
weathers to be sure he gets the picture he wants …even when the police ask
him to, "Move along, son."

In his visionary quest – his labour of love – he says that it's a lonely life
being a photographer – just him and his camera. Paul, who has travelled the
world on commissions and projects to the Far and Middle East and America,
believes that despite the glamour there's no place like home.

A good picture is like a great joke, he stresses: the timing; structure;
observation and delivery – all working towards a laugh…or a sigh … or
a cry at the end of it. He gets letters from all over the globe from people
who treasure his images. In this book you will see that his years of hard
graft and dedication and professionalism has brought great recognition and
success. Why? Because he gives YOU the picture – the rest is up to YOUR
imagination. Good photographers all agree – the audience work just as hard
as the person who takes the picture in the first place.

Enjoy this collection of Liverpool then and Liverpool now – as seen through
the eyes and lens of Paul McMullin who is as much in love with his home
town as you are.

INTRODUCTION

Following on from *Portrait of Liverpool 2004* and *Liverpool the Great City 2009* this updated and revised version explores old favourites and the new architecture of a city that has been transformed over the last 10 years.

I still find the city a fascinating place to wander around. Early mornings, whether it be winter or summer in Liverpool, have an almost magical feel to the quality of light and this is my favourite time of day. However, wandering around the city at any time is worthwhile for photography. When looking, the new buildings, the refurbishment of existing buildings or just seeing old favourites at different times, a detail of a building is picked out by a shaft of light, or perhaps, a complete building is illuminated against a stormy sky. We may well be second only to London in terms of the number of listed buildings, but for me it is a city that lends itself to photography! Some buildings I re-visit once again, it is certainly not possible to leave these icons out of a book on Liverpool. The old favourites – the Three Graces (The Liver Building, Cunard Building and the Port of Liverpool Building), St George's Hall, the two cathedrals, Liverpool Cathedral (Anglican) and The Metropolitan Cathedral of Christ the King (Roman Catholic) and The Albert Dock to name just a few. I was also fortunate enough to be able to photograph the Minton tiled floor in St George's Hall in January; this truly magnificent scene is only occasionally revealed!

The area around the waterfront now has World Heritage Status and there are new developments: Liverpool One, the 42 acre redevelopment of Paradise Street and South John Street. Additionally, Chevasse Park now links the city centre with the waterfront and The Albert Dock plus the new Echo Arena and BT Conference Centre. The land in front of the Three Graces, known locally as the Pier Head, has been totally redesigned, incorporating an extension to the Leeds–Liverpool canal which links Canning Dock and the Albert Dock. A new £10.5m Pier Head Ferry Terminal, and slightly further to the north on Prince's Parade a cruise liner terminal, now enables large passenger ships to berth alongside for the first time since the late 1960s with 'Turnaround' capability.

The distinctive new builds on the Mann Island site, (the area between the Pier Head and the Albert Dock) are now complete and these buildings, together with those set further back from the waterfront, such as Unity Building, 20 Chapel Street and West Tower, have all combined to change the shape of the Liverpool Waterfront. I believe it is now a truly magnificent 21st century city – A Waterfront City.

While revising, and hopefully improving the content for this book, we looked again at the buildings to be included or re-photographed, the layout was refreshed as, in the three years since the first edition was published, there have been significant changes to the city whether for the better or not – some like the juxtaposition of the new buildings alongside the Graces, some not! It is a personal and subjective view. Mike McNamee has once again put the text to my images. This book is really dedicated to those people living in the city and to those people who have moved away and have connections either spiritual or physical, but also to those visiting the city for the first time. Therefore there will be views and buildings not included which one may argue, should be, but conversely we hope that we there are images of buildings that are often overlooked, which have been included.

When exploring the city, get out, enjoy its sights and, as my first employer, Richard Cooper of Photoflex used to say, 'Look up' as there is a wealth of history, interest and architecture above our heads.

Paul McMullin June 2012

The *Queen Mary 2* is berthed at the Cruise Liner Terminal in September 2011. The Three Graces are built on the site of the old, George's Dock. The Albert Dock may be seen just to the right of the new Museum of Liverpool.

The cathedrals (top of the picture) mark the border between the city centre and the outlying suburbs.

THE WATERFRONT

This annotated panorama shows the principal buildings of the Liverpool Waterfront.

- Alexandra Tower
- City Lofts Apartments
- Beetham Tower
- West Tower
- The Capital (formerly The Royal Insurance Building)
- Malmaison Hotel
- Unity Building
- 20 Chapel Street
- The Atlantic Tower Hotel
- St John's Beacon
- The Church of Our Lady & St Nicholas Tower

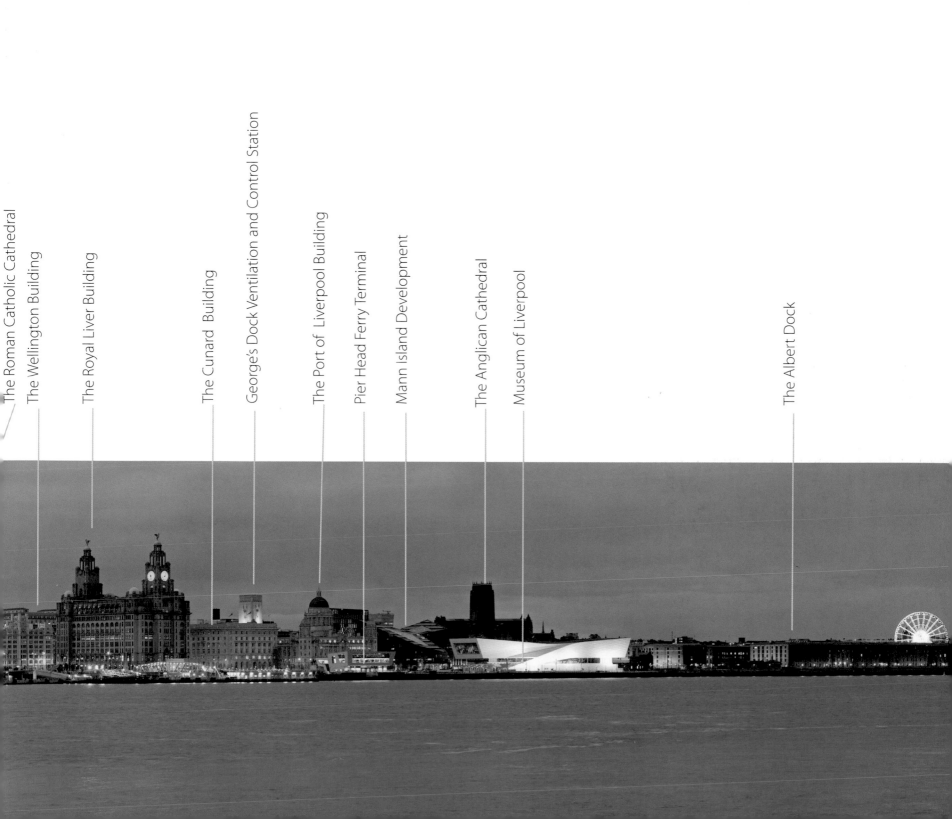

The Roman Catholic Cathedral

The Wellington Building

The Royal Liver Building

The Cunard Building

George's Dock Ventilation and Control Station

The Port of Liverpool Building

Pier Head Ferry Terminal

Mann Island Development

The Anglican Cathedral

Museum of Liverpool

The Albert Dock

CHAPTER 1

THE WATERFRONT

Liverpool's development has been dominated by its deep-water, river frontage, the Waterfront. It was not always so and in earlier centuries the main port of the area was Parkgate on the River Dee. Liverpool slowly took the prominent position as the Dee silted up and ships became larger. To a local, the Waterfront is regarded as the area around the Three Graces – the Royal Liver Building, the Cunard Building and the Port of Liverpool Building. The skyline takes into view other buildings behind the docks and is bounded to the north by Alexandra Tower and to the south by the Anglican Cathedral. The Waterfront is somewhat disconnected from the city by the Strand, a busy eight-lane road. The name echoes its past as the original promenade, before the massive dock walls were built to harness the tides.

As a view, the Waterfront is best enjoyed from the famous Mersey Ferries, either from onboard or after you have landed at the Woodside or Wallasey Terminals. From there you can take in the whole expanse, centred on the Three Graces, but extending as far as the eye can see in either direction. The skyline has changed dramatically over the past few years and in particular as the 'Big Dig' has been completed. Those of us who live on the Wirral side enjoy much the best view of the Waterfront with an uninterrupted view all the way from New Brighton down to Woodside.

The importance of the skyline is possibly greatest for the sailors who have made their way into the port over the centuries. The skyline tells them they are home, the familiarity of the outline defines their safe arrival. This has particular resonance for the dwindling number who sailed into the port, battered and bruised by the North Atlantic Convoys of World War II. How their brothers, lost at sea, would marvel at the famous skyline were they able to see it today.

"...made from hammered copper plates, bolted together on an armature..."

One of the two famous Liver Birds which stand over 100 metres above the city, on top of the clock towers of the Royal Liver Building. One faces into the city while the other faces across the Mersey to the Wirral. Each bird is identical and they stand six metres high. The heads are just over a metre in length and the wings are three metres long. The mythical birds are made of hammered copper plates, bolted together on a structure of rolled steel joints. The designer was Carl Bernard Bartels (1866 – 1955) and the maker was George Cowper and the Bromsgrove Guild. During the xenophobia of the First World War, Bartels' contribution was erased from the records because he was of German origin; he was interred on the Isle of Man. The vapour trails are from over-passing flights en route to London or Europe which has passed over the Wallasey navigation beacon.

The Port of Liverpool building was the first of the
Three Graces to be built (1903 – 1907) and was the
headquarters of the Mersey Docks and Harbour Board.
The symmetrical building is a steel structure, encased in
concrete and faced with Portland Stone. The interior of
the central dome is a magnificent space, encircled with
the quotation, "They that go down to the sea in ships,
that do business in great waters. These see the works of
the LORD and his wonders in the deep".

LIVERPOOL The Great City

"…Ferries have crossed the Mersey for centuries, starting around 1396. …"

PREVIOUS PAGES LEFT:
The Royal Liver Building seen from Water St. The ornate lanterns on the left are fixed to the India Buildings, designed by Herbert Rowse in 1923 and originally the offices of Alfred Holt Ltd, which sailed ships under the Blue Funnel Line name from 1865 and latterly became the Ocean Steamship Company. The famous Liver clocks, in the distance, are 25 feet in diameter. Three clocks face the river, the fourth (shown here) faces into the city.

PREVIOUS PAGES RIGHT:
The high-rise towers are a new feature of the Liverpool skyline. West Tower is seen between the rear of the Cunard Building and the George's Dock ventilation shaft for the Mersey Tunnel – a span of more than 100 years of architectural development.

LEFT:
The new Pier Head Ferry Terminal. Opened in May 2009, it includes a café, restaurant, and visitor centre. Ferries have crossed the Mersey for centuries, starting around 1396.

THIS PAGE:
A view from Mann Island of the Pier Head, Waterfront buildings. With the ever-present West Tower looming in the background.

ABOVE:
The Cunard Building was the last of the Three Graces to be completed in 1916. It was the head quarters of the Cunard Shipping Line and served as both offices and as a passenger terminal. Its design has now been attributed to Arthur J Davis, of Mewès and Davis.

RIGHT:
The Royal Liver Building of 1908–11 was designed to weather gracefully in the smoke of the time. It was restored to its original, pristine condition, almost a hundred years later. It was the second of the Three Graces to be constructed, basically of concrete reinforced with steel, with an exterior cladding of granite. The construction technique allowed the 10 main storeys to be built at an average rate of one floor every nineteen working days. The new canal link shows in the foreground.

ABOVE:
A shot taken from Bidston Hill on the Wirral, (a distance of 3.3 miles), at the original spot where flags would be raised to alert the merchants in Liverpool of the imminent arrival of their ships. They could then arrange stevedores while the vessels sailed through the Burbo Bank off the Wirral and shortly to dock at the port.

RIGHT:
The return of large cruise-liners to Liverpool signals a resurgence of the city as a tourist destination. MV *Grand Princess* is in the process of being turned mid river prior to departure and The *Queen Mary 2* is berthed at the Cruise Liner Terminal which has now been accorded 'Turnaround' status meaning that cruises can start and end once again in Liverpool.
Note the height of tide demonstrated by the fact that the pier head landing stage is almost horizontal. Liverpool has a 31 foot tidal range. The Proudman Institute has moved from Bidston Hall on the Wirral to a new building in the city. It is famed for the studies on tidal patterns.

LEFT:
The telephoto lens from on board the Mersey Ferry has compressed the architectural heritage of the Waterfront into a single frame.

23

ABOVE:
Italian Renaissance detail on the frieze of the Cunard
Building reflects the oppulence of the first-class
passenger lounge from which passengers embarked,
whereas lower class passengers were accommodated
in the basement, along with baggage handling and
storage.

ABOVE:
Canals return to the city. The Leeds-Liverpool Canal was intended to bring the goods of Lancashire industries to the port. This fell into decline with the emergence of the railways, but the waterway was recently re-opened and extended all the way to the Albert Dock. The re-opened Liverpool lock system brings narrow boats into Stanley Dock from where they can cruise onwards to the West Waterloo Dock, then Prince's Dock and across the front of the Three Graces, eventually arriving into the Albert Dock.

The flight of the locks at Wigan restricts the length of narrow boats compared with the standard for the rest of the UK. The 'Liverpool Short Boat' is 62 foot long but wider than normal at 14' 4" beam. Traditional Midlands craft cannot sail west of Wigan.

The George's Dock Ventilation Tower by Herbert Rowse. The two statues, in black basalt, signify night and day to reflect the 24-hour operation of the Mersey Tunnel. The motorcyclist represents a modern Mercury, complete with racing helmet and goggles. One of the original toll booths now stands at the foot of the building – these were replaced by automatic barriers.

"...It was designed by two-times winner of the RIBA Stirling Prize for architecture, Wilkinson Eyre. ..."

The Echo Arena and BT Convention Centre occupies the site on the King's Dock adjacent to the Albert Dock and overlooked by the Anglican Cathedral. It was designed by two-times winner of the RIBA Stirling Prize for architecture, Wilkinson Eyre.

ABOVE:
The Strand was originally a promenade directly on the seafront. The dock-building, and the height of walls needed to provide draught clearance for the ships moved the wharves and warehouses to the seaward side. Warehouses once occupied the middle of this busy thoroughfare (The Goree being the road on the right in this picture, with the Strand on its left).

ABOVE:
The new Pier Head Ferry Terminal. Opened in May 2009 includes a café, gift shop cinema and visitor centre with a Beatles Exhibition. On the top level is *Matou-Pan* Asian Restaurant.

ABOVE and LEFT:
Two aerial views of the now complete Mann Island Development showing neatly how the new buildings form a geodetic pattern but contrast sharply with the ornate Pier Head designs from early last century however they work in harmony with each other.

PREVIOUS PAGE LEFT:
The Three Graces are relatively isolated when viewed from the air though very close to the Cruise Liner Terminal and the Albert Dock. The new canal section is linked through tunnels across from the Prince's Dock to the Albert Dock (on the right). The city extends backwards towards Aigburth and then onwards to Speke, John Lennon International Airport and the Manchester Ship Canal.

On a cold winter's morning The Royal Liver Building is shrouded by mist; the public art, in Hope Street, reflects something of Liverpool's historical status as a centre for both immigration and emigration.

CHAPTER 2

THE ARCHITECTURAL HERITAGE

Although Liverpool suffered extensive bomb damage in 1941, the majority of significant buildings survived the devastation. Most of the buildings reflect the size and importance of the port, the majority of the land being taken over by docks, warehousing and commercial premises. By way of example, Liverpool University has only existed since 1903.

The drive for commercialism within and around the city means that only a single pre-eighteenth century building survives. The majority of the architecture is late Georgian, Victorian and Edwardian, built on a massive scale, which reflects the stature of the dock walls, designed to hold back the 30-foot tides. The first commercial, enclosed dock in the world was opened here in 1715.

The Blue Coat School (now The Bluecoat) was built in 1716 –18. Abolition of the slave trade in 1807 did not produce the expected demise of the port; more docks were built and the revenue increased many-fold. Between 1830 and 1930, nine million emigrants passed through Liverpool, some stayed and never travelled onwards!

The isolation of the port from its hinterland was relieved firstly by the spate of canal building, then with the completion of the world's first railway. Lime Street station was finished in 1836. St George's Hall soon followed on the land opposite, opening in 1854. In 1886 the Mersey Railway linked the Wirral with the port via the tunnel under the Mersey.

Without question it is the buildings around the Pier Head that are the most well known and provided a welcome sight for the convoys of Second World War shipping battling home through packs of U-boats. That was really the last act of major traffic to the actual Port of Liverpool and by the mid-'70s the south docks lay as a silent witness to the times that preceded it.

Initially Liverpool developed very rapidly as a commercial centre and many buildings were simply knocked down when they impeded progress. It is therefore ironic that the Albert Dock has risen from the dereliction and is now the UK's third busiest tourist attraction.

Development has been rekindled with the modification of the architectural heritage for other uses (mainly housing and leisure). Some of the newer buildings are exciting and adventurous in their design, especially those alongside the Three Graces providing a continuing link to the older, equally adventurous building of the late 1800s and early 1900s. Liverpool became the European Capital of Culture in 2008, a prestige that was accompanied by a spate of building, typified by Liverpool One. Liverpool - Maritime Mercantile City was inscribed as a cultural World Heritage Site by the UNESCO World Heritage Committee on 2 July 2004.

RIGHT: The Bluecoat.

Liverpool Town Hall is situated between Dale Street,
Castle Street, Water Street and High Street, in the heart
of the business district. Designed by John Wood, the
building was opened in 1754, with various changes
and revisions being made throughout the next 40
years. In 1795 the building was devastated by fire and
was quickly rebuilt with the central dome completed
in 1802 and the projecting portico (at the front, facing
down Castle Street), completed in 1811.

> **" ...modern thinking sides with Britannia but the records are inconclusive... "**

The statue astride of the dome of the Town Hall is either Britannia or Minerva – modern thinking sides with Britannia but the records are inconclusive. She was erected in 1801–02.

Little remains of the original market and exchange other than the enclosed space of Exchange Flags. Much business was transacted in this open space and the nearby Corn Exchange. The memorial stands to Nelson's four victories at Cape St Vincent, the Nile, Copenhagen and Trafalgar. The statue was publicly funded in the aftermath of Nelson's death and almost £9,000 was raised in just over two months.

The view down North John Street, towards the golden cupola of the former Royal Insurance building of 1896-1903. It was built using a steel frame technique and is possibly one of the first in this country designed in this way.

St George's Hall and Plateau, completed in 1839, is the second largest building in the city, giving way only to the Anglican Cathedral. It was built at a cost of £30,000 and includes a large public space (ball room), a small concert room, an assize (crown) court and a civil court. The design was the result of a competition won by Harvey Lonsdale Elmes and pioneered a heating and ventilation solution with a water fountain used to clean the air before it was re-introduced to the building. In 1969 the architectural historian Nikolaus Pevsner expressed his opinion that it is one of the finest neo-Grecian buildings in the world although the building is notable for its use of Roman sources as well as Greek ones. In 2004 the hall and its surrounding area were recognised as part of Liverpool's World Heritage Site.

The interior of St George's Hall.
The Minton floor tiles at St George's Concert Hall in Liverpool are normally covered by a protective flooring. The 30,000 hand-crafted Minton tiles, made in the English Potteries, are also used in the USA for the Capitol Building and the White House (as well as the Princes Road Synagogue) and were laid in 1852 to provide a hard surface for dancing These images were made in January 2012. Previously they were last uncovered in early 2009. In 1954 when the tiles were uncovered over 100,000 people queued to see the floor. The reverse view is taken from the balcony around the console of the great organ. The doors at the far end are the division between the Hall and the Assize Court.

**" …often cases
were of only
six minutes
duration
and in effect
there was a
production line
mentality…"**

The Assize Court inside the St George's Hall.
The original design competition was for both
new courts and a public building. Harvey
Lonsdale Elmes won both competitions and
combined the designs into a single building.
The court had a reputation for fast delivery of
justice, often cases were of only six minutes
duration and in effect there was a production
line mentality.

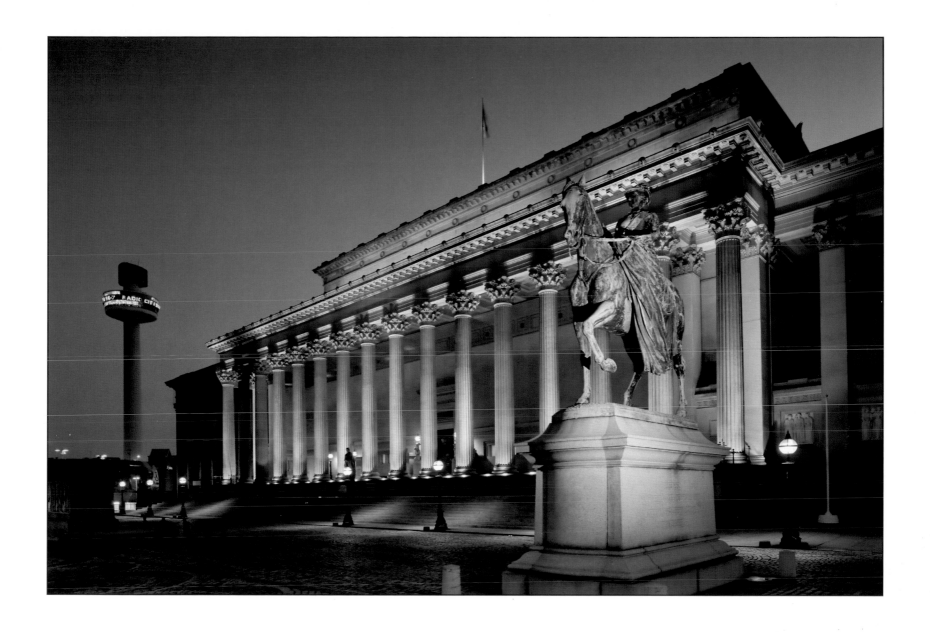

Outside the front of the building, Queen Victoria rides side-saddle and is wearing a ribband of the Order of St George. The statue was ordered in bronze but following concerns of the Liverpool Corporation's surveyor as to its condition it was subsequently admitted by the foundry that it was made of gun metal. It required restorative work in 1885, just 15 years after installation.

ABOVE:
The small Concert Room was completed in 1856, two years after the main hall.

LEFT:
The rear of St George's Hall. Many say that this should have been the front aspect of the building, with the beautiful St John's Gardens leading up to an entrance, however, this never materialised (see page 62-63).

Major General William Earle seems to point the visitors towards Wellington. Earle was killed while leading the rescue of Gordon, at Khartoum, taking an enemy bullet to the head. The statue was paid for by public subscriptions that were limited to two guineas (to encourage inclusiveness) and the monument was erected in December 1887. The Wellington Column was erected in 1863. It used to be possible to climb up to the top using internal stairs and the rails were secured for VE Day, in 1945, with scaffold poles. They remain there to this day as a memento of the occasion. A standard yard is sculpted into the base plaque.

A view from the entrance of St George's Hall towards
the North Western Hotel, a seven floor, 330-room
building, opened in 1871. Adjacent to the Lime Street
rail terminal, this important stopping place now houses
students for Liverpool John Moores University.

The Lime Street Gateway Concourse was completed in 2010. It was designed by Glenn Howells Architects.

Recently refurbished, Liverpool Lime Street station was an engineering feat of its day, the first fully-iron engine shed. The iron structure spans 200 feet and was constructed in 1879, the third station on the site in 40 years. When constructed in 1867 it had the largest span in the world but was almost immediately stripped of its title by St Pancras station in London. The second shed was added ten years later.

The most recent addition are statues of two Liverpool legends, Ken Dodd and Bessie Braddock. Bessie holds the 'Lion' branded egg, Doddy his trademark 'tickling stick'.

The cobbled carriageway leads past the recently-renamed Liverpool Museum, now World Museum, the Hornby Library and Picton Reading Room, Walker Art Gallery and the County Sessions House.

Michelangelo was sculpted by John Warrington Wood in Rome in 1877. He sits at the entrance to the Walker Art Gallery opposite another statue by Warrington, this time of Raphael.

RIGHT:
The Picton Reading Room, by Cornelius Sherlock (1875–9). Lit with electricity from the start (although gas was installed as a back-up) by three lamps in the circular dish in the centre of the room. It is 30 metres in diameter, with the original wrought iron galleries running the full circumference of the building.

Interior views of The Walker Art Gallery and the splendid marble section.

The aerial view shows the County Sessions House, Walker Art Gallery, Hornby Library and Picton Reading Room, and World Museum in the foreground. The circular end of St George's Hall holds the small concert room. Lime Street station can be seen behind the North Western Hotel.

"...Martins Bank by HJ Rowse "probably the best example of 20th Century American style classicism"... "

LEFT:
The interior of the former Martins Bank.

RIGHT:
Every detail, right down to the stationery holders was overseen by the architect, Herbert Rowse.

FAR RIGHT:
The eighth-floor board room.

RIGHT TOP:
The view down Water Street towards the Pier Head across the front of Martins Bank and the Town Hall.

PREVIOUS PAGE:
Oriel Chambers on the left, the delightful, airy office space, designed to illuminate the office workers' desks from three sides. Behind this is 20 Chapel Street, which is a mixed commercial and residential development which dominates Chapel Street. With its mosaic of panels, 20 Chapel Street forms part of the Unity development, which is now a dominant feature of the Liverpool skyline.

THIS PAGE:
Peter Ellis also designed 16 Cook Street where he expanded on his use of glass for Oriel Chambers. Surprisingly open, and an exuberance of glass for a building erected in 1866, the interior contains a fine set of cast iron steps.

Parts of the city await restoration. This is the Pig and Whistle public house in Chapel St. The port was famous for its pubs, some roads having almost one on every corner. They formed meeting places for dockers as they waited the arrival of ships and provided a place for gathering news of opportunities for work. Between pub and church comes James Picton's Hargreaves Building (1859). The carved plaques above the windows depict famous people who were involved in exploration of the New World, an apt theme for one of the great staging ports for the Americas.

> **❝…gradually the old is being pulled down to make way for the new, watched over by _Enterprise_…❞**

The statue of _Enterprise_, erected to the memory of Sir Alfred Lewis Jones, a Liverpool shipowner who, together with members of the business community, founded Liverpool School of Tropical Medicine in 1898, the first of its kind in the world. Between 1898 and 1913 the School despatched no fewer than 32 expeditions to the tropics, including Sierra Leone, the Democratic Republic of Congo and South America.

Albion House (White Star Line Building or Oceanic House) built in 1898 and designed by Richard Norman Shaw is very similar in design to New Scotland Yard in London. It was commissioned by J B Ismay the owner of the White Star Line whose office was situated in the bottom right-hand turret. It was from this building, that the list of survivors from the *Titanic* disaster were announced to crowds gathered on the Strand waiting for news . A poignant reminder of that fateful day in April1912.

The building has a Grade II* listed status and although the interior was modernised in the 1970s and 1980s with false ceilings and partitions, the exterior is remarkably unchanged except for an externally mounted clock and a simpler top gable end which was replaced after war damage. Currently the building is unoccupied.

Herbert Rowse designed the George's Dock Ventilation and Control Centre for the Mersey Road Tunnel which was opened by King V in July 1934. (See pages 28 and 29 for other features of this fine example of an Art Deco building.) It was reconstructed under the supervision of Rowse during 1951–2 following war damage. The red and white building (centre right) is another view of Albion House. This view is no longer possible with the recent addition of a Travel Lodge hotel on the Strand, an interesting comparison of new and old architecture.

LEFT:
The Liverpool One scheme has used its historical
roots to highlight the site of the old dock designed by
William Hutchinson.

ABOVE:
The original Steers Dock of 1765 has been excavated
and is open to the public for viewing. The viewing
window situated adjacent to the John Lewis store gives
little indication of what actually lies beneath the street.

CHAPTER 2 The Architectural Heritage   **73**

> **"** …once the rich dwelling place of the sea captains… **"**

Gambier Terrance was once a prime housing location, providing rich dwelling places for the sea captains of the port. Built in 1836, it has a commanding view of the Anglican Cathedral.

The Anglican Cathedral towers above the Georgian streets.

PREVIOUS PAGE:
Rodney Street, often described as the Harley Street of Liverpool, with its many medical specialists. Number 59 once housed the Liverpool photographer, E Chambré Hardman and the house is now a museum to this local artist, owned and run by The National Trust.

LEFT:
Jacob Epstein's famous male figure on the outside of the Lewis's department store (commonly known as 'Dickie Lewis'). Its unveiling in November 1956 was accompanied by 'a murmur of approval' although it was far from universally praised. The figure signifies the struggle for resurgence of Liverpool after the blitz of 3 May 1941 which almost completely destroyed the original building.

LIVERPOOL The Great City

LEFT:
The Victoria Building of 1889–92 on Brownlow Hill was
the main teaching and administrative building of the
newly-formed university college. It was the inspiration
of the term 'red-brick university' and is now the
Victoria Gallery and Museum. The recently remodelled
University Square is in the foreground.

ABOVE:
The interior of the VG&M. Here the Waterhouse café
on the ground floor. The first and second floors house
the art collections and museum.

CHAPTER 3

THE CATHEDRALS AND CHURCHES

For a city with such a wealthy history Liverpool has very few churches. Much of the architecture was dominated by the commercial need to warehouse the vast quantities of goods being delivered into the port. The crowning glories of the city's ecclesiastical architecture are its two cathedrals. Although they are joined by the same street, in an architectural sense they are as far apart as they could be. The Anglican Cathedral, dedicated to St James, was started in 1904 with the city at its peak of prosperity and was finished in 1978 when the long decline was at its lowest point. The building is massive in scale, the largest Anglican Cathedral in Christendom. It shares the other end of Hope Street with the Roman Catholic Metropolitan Cathedral, itself a building of remarkable design with a centre altar and a congregation of 2,000 seated in a sweeping arc around it.

The other churches are somewhat dwarfed by the scale of the cathedrals but there are some architectural gems dotted about the city. The Greek Orthodox Church of St Nicholas is outstanding and just visible above the Waterfront skyline. Its decorative brickwork is an echo of Shaw's Albion House, itself modelled on his own New Scotland Yard building. It is actually a close copy of the St Theodore Church in Constantinople. Also noteworthy is the Swedish Seaman's Church (1884), a riot of brickwork windows, arches and spires. The Princes Road Synagogue is also a religious building of considerable importance.

The denominations of the churches reflects the mix of people who moved into the city to find work. Although many think of Liverpool as a suburb of Ireland, there were an almost equal number of Welsh labourers and their families. This is reflected in the churches; by 1891 the census shows 26 Roman Catholic and 27 'Welsh' churches. A generalised demarcation is that Irish labour manned the docksides and Welsh labour, the warehouses. Wales also provided quite a number of skilled building trades' people and the regular packet steamers to Llandudno provided a link with their homes and families.

The Metropolitan Cathedral of Christ the King.

The interior layout of the cathedral reflects the exterior design in that the seating and side altars are based on a circular pattern.

The Lutyen's Crypt, the only surviving part of Edwin Lutyen's grand design for the second largest cathedral in the world. War and rising costs saw the original plan scrapped and all that remains of the idea is a model in the Museum of Liverpool at Mann Island (see page 120).

Lutyen's bold move for grandeur was replaced by the
adventurous design of Sir Frederick Gibberd. Work
began in 1962 and the building was consecrated
in 1967. Today it is flanked on the far side by the
new Liverpool University Arts Building designed by
Rick Mather and by the two Liverpool Science Park
buildings.

LIVERPOOL FEMALE ORPHAN ASYLUM.

Ann Davis,	Aged 11 years, Died 26. May 1844.
Alice Buckley,	Aged 9 years, Died 9. April 1845.
Ann Ellis,	Aged 10 years, Died 16. June 1846.
Elizth Williams,	Aged 13 years, Died 2. May 1847.
Sarah B. Moss,	Aged 10 years, Died 13. May 1847.
Marg^t Hegan,	Aged 8 years, Died 30. May 1847.
Charlotte Boyd,	Aged 11 years, Died 18. April 1849.
Ann Sumner,	Aged 9 years, Died 30. Novr 1849.
Elizth Hughes,	Aged 11 years, Died 22. June 1850.
Jane E. Garner,	Aged 14 years, Died 28. Augt 1850.

LEFT:
The Anglican Cathedral was started in time to lay the foundation stone in 1904 and completed 74 years later on 25 October 1978. It is a huge building, the Lady Chapel at the lower right is larger than most parish churches and is an architectural jewel in its own right. It has the largest and heaviest peal of bells in the world. The tower rises to more than 330 feet. The building is 619 feet in length. Examining the old photographs of the construction shows relatively few workmen, never more than ten in any one picture. Despite this they laid a little short of five million bricks! The image shown was taken in the first few seconds of 2008, the start of Liverpool's year as European Capital of Culture.

ABOVE:
The gravestones of the adjacent St James' Cemetery are a lasting memorial to the many who died in the crowded, unsanitary conditions of the mid-nineteenth century. This example is to the orphaned girls who died – none reached the age of 15 years. Liverpool pioneered a number of intitiatives to assist the poor and improve their daily lives. Wash-houses, The Bluecoat School, workshops for the blind, institutes for the deaf and dumb, the public health movement and many others originated in the city.

“…A cathedral fit for a city of
the stature of Liverpool…”

Bishop Chavasse

PREVIOUS PAGE:
From the air the immense scale of the cathedral is more apparent. Gambier Terrace flanks the right-hand side in the picture. The housing, offices and university complex, to the left of the cathedral in the picture, have been sympathetically designed. The St James' gardens surround the cathedral on three sides. There is a sloping promenade down to the gardens which contain many grave stones and the Huskisson Memorial. He was a local MP and the first fatal casualty of the railway era, being knocked down on the opening day of the Liverpool–Manchester railway and later dying of his injuries.

TOP RIGHT:
The memorial stone to Kitty Wilkinson, the founder of the first public Wash House in 1842 after outbreaks of cholera in 1832 and 1840.

MIDDLE:
The Oratory, situated adjacent to the cathedral. This is the former mortuary chapel to St James' Cemetery and was designed by John Foster Jr in the style of a Greek Doric Temple. Built 1829.

BOTTOM RIGHT:
The Ramps. Another design by John Foster Jr, intended to allow funeral processions to descend into the cemetery and for the mourners to promenade. The Huskisson Memorial can be seen right. John Foster Jr was a prominent Liverpool corporation surveyor b1786 d1846. He is also buried here.

The two great cathedrals of Liverpool
are joined by Hope Street at a distance
of about half a mile.

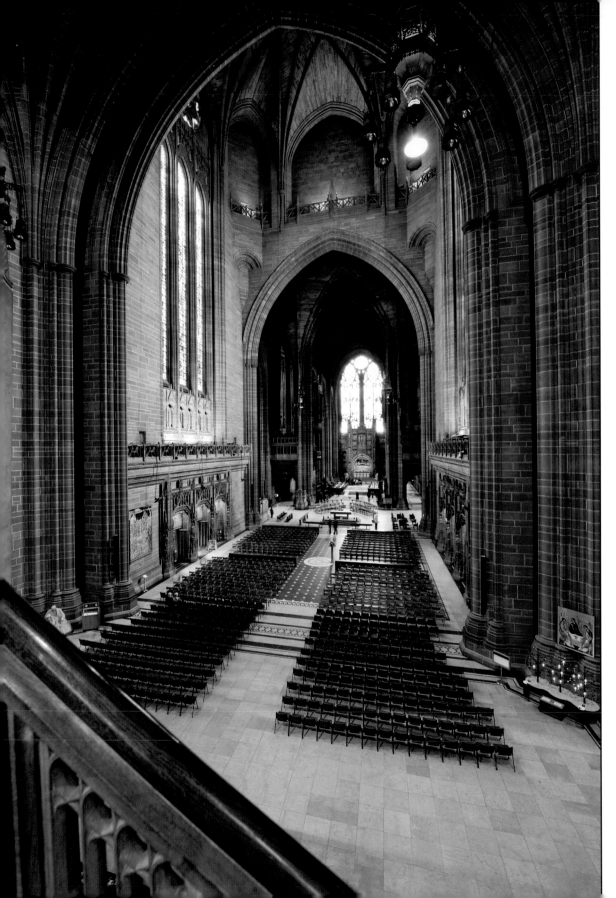

The interior of the cathedral is relatively plain and uncluttered, giving a great sense of space. The chair arrangement may be varied to suit the church-service requirements and a huge open lift can take them down to an underground store.

The Church of Our Lady and St Nicholas Tower. Built 1811–1815. The nave was rebuilt in 1952 because of war damage. In 1810 the original (1774) church also suffered a bizarre accident when the tower collapsed under the weight of the pealing bells and fell onto the Sunday congregation below. Twenty-three girls from the Moorefield's Charity School died in the incident.

LEFT:
Liverpool has played host to many nationalities, ethnicities and religions. The Chinese Archway was constructed by Chinese craftspeople in 2000. The local China Town is one of the oldest in the country, more than a century in the city. The arch stands alongside the Great George Street Congregational Church (1840–1), locally known as the 'Blackie'. Recently refurbished it is still known as the 'Black E' and is a centre for the arts and the community.

THIS PAGE:
Always known as the 'bombed out church'. The Church of St Luke stands at the top of Bold Street and Berry Street. Built by the corporation under the auspicies of John Foster Sr, around about 1805. It was eventually completed by John Foster Jr in 1827 who succeeded his father as corporation surveyor. The church serves as a war memorial.

LIVERPOOL The Great City

> **"**...it provided a wholesome but attractive alternative to pub and music hall...**"**

LEFT:
The Metropolitan Cathedral sits at the top of Brownlow Hill and, like the Anglican Cathedral on St James' Mount, it can be seen clearly across the city. The domed building in the foreground is the Central Hall of the Liverpool Wesleyan Mission.

THIS PAGE:
Central Hall was opened in 1905; its main auditorium seated almost 2,500 people. It provided a wholesome but attractive alternative to pub and music hall with concerts and other social activities. It is a most unchurch-like building, now occupied by the famous Quiggins collective of traders and shops. It was designed by Bradshaw and Gass of Bolton.

LIVERPOOL The Great City

The Princes Road Synagogue has been described as one of the finest examples of Orientalism in British synagogue architecture. The view that greets the visitor as they enter the central doors is quite astounding. The ornate Bitmah (reading platform) leads on towards the Pulpit, behind which stands an Ark, decorated in polished red granite and crowned with five, deep blue domes, which are in turn, decorated with gold stars. The lower levels reflect a heavy 'moorish' influence in the design while the rose windows at either end are typically European in design, if not in their geometric detail. This Grade 1 listed building was the design of the brothers, W and G Audsley and it opened in 1874 as the finest example of their work. The building costs were substantially contributed by David Lewis (of the Lewis' Department Store) but the community has contributed much to the local arts, political and business life. As a staging post towards America, a great many Russo-Polish Jews came to Liverpool and got no further – their descendants still form part of the present congregations.

"…He who has not seen the interior of Princes Road Synagogue in Liverpool has not beheld the glory of Israel…." H.A. Meek (1993)

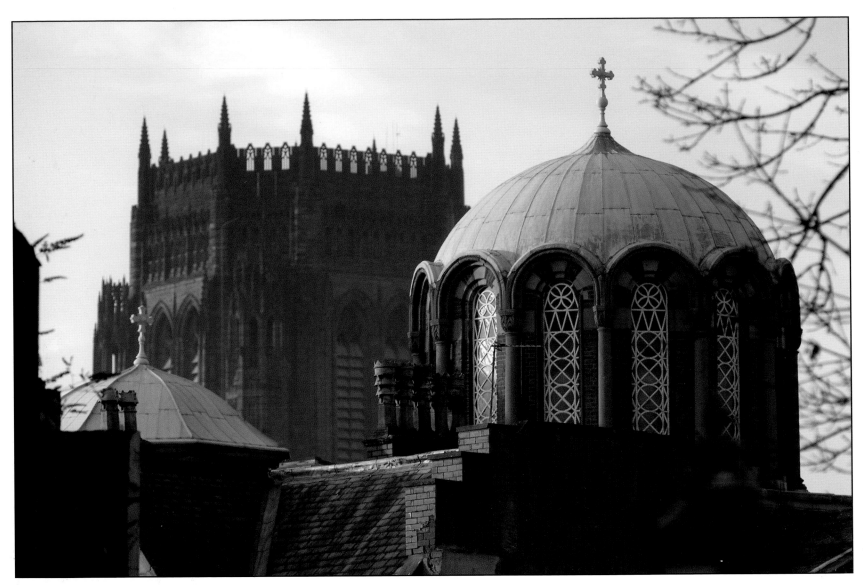

ABOVE:
The Greek Orthodox Church, which was built in 1870, is situated just a few yards along Princes Road from the synagogue. The 'Welsh Presbyterian Cathedral' is situated a little further up the road as is the Roman Catholic Church of St Margaret to complete this cluster of religious buildings.

LEFT:
The *Gustav Adolfs Kyrka* known locally as the 'Swedish Seaman's Church'. Built in 1883–4.

RIGHT:
The former St Peter's Catholic Church on the south side of Seel Street. The church was opened on 7 September 1788. It served as a catholic church for 188 years. In 1976, it was transferred to the Polish Community and it is still referred to as 'the Polish Church'. It held its last service in 1978. It is now *Alma de Cuba*, a very upmarket restaurant and bar. It was the first church building in Liverpool to be turned into a social venue.

CHAPTER 4

LEISURE AND TOURISM

There are many facets to the status of Liverpool as a tourism and leisure city. The Albert Dock is a World Heritage Centre and a major attraction but, in the main, people do not come to the city just to admire Jesse Hartley's 'pile of bricks'. It is, however, of such importance that it has its own chapter at the end of this book.

To the outsider, the city is most closely associated with music and football, it is rare that a local has to explain in detail where they are from when visiting any other part of the world. Historically, Liverpool has received an eclectic mix of cultures and races because of its prominent position as a seaport and staging post to the far reaches of the old empire. The tourist mix therefore comprises those who are returning to their roots and those who are curious to see just where Lennon, McCartney, Starr and Harrison hung out. One of the most frequent comments the natives of the city hear is that their guests cannot believe what a handsome city Liverpool is. The Waterfront, viewed from either the other side of the Mersey, or from the famous Mersey Ferry, is a spectacular sight and one of the aims of this book has been to illustrate just how much it has changed since our fore-runner book, *A Portrait of Liverpool* was published.

Good tourist destinations need a mixture of attractions, including shops. Liverpool has two impressive cathedrals, a wonderful collection of public buildings, a waterfront, museums, galleries but, until recently had lagged a little on the shopping front. The concept for Liverpool One was to provide a new shopping district which linked the major attractions of the Waterfront to the city centre, nightlife and cathedrals. This was accomplished by appointing a single overseeing developer (from 47 applicants) who then proceeded to engage the services of a large number of architectural practices, who were effectively cut loose to be as creative as possible. The only stipulation was that a covered mall was not permissible. Liverpool One has achieved almost all of its aims. The Albert Dock is now just a stone's throw from the start of the shopping area of Liverpool One and this provides a natural conduit into the rest of the city.

Any large city is something like an onion. At the core are the major attractions, the Beatles Experience, the Mersey Ferry, the Three Graces, the cathedrals. Outside of this there are the gems that only the enthusiastic traveller gets to – the galleries, the UK's second largest collection of public statues, the churches of other denominations, China Town, the list could go on and on.

Liverpool One from the air.

LEFT:
The Liverpool skyline behind the silhouetted figure of Anthony Gormley's *Another Place*. This inventive piece of public art covers a mile-long stretch of the coastline just to the north of the Seaforth Dock, with identical cast iron figures, set at various locations on the beach. They are a local attraction, frequently decorated with scarves and clothing by the residents and visitors.

RIGHT:
The Liverpool Big Wheel. The 60 metre high tourist attraction is positioned on the piazza outside the Liverpool Echo Arena and Convention Centre – near to the Albert Dock.

The wheel includes 42 fully enclosed, air-conditioned capsules offering riders spectacular panoramic views of the city, the River Mersey, the Welsh mountains and the World Heritage Site waterfront.

ABOVE:
The Liverpool Sailors' Home gateway originally stood on the site of the current John Lewis building just to the left of this picture. It is now loacted at the end of Paradise Street.

RIGHT:
An unusual view of the Big Wheel (it really doesn't go that quickly!). However, this view allows us to see the Albert Dock complex in the foreground with Mann Island and The Pier Head in the distance.

LEFT:
Liverpool One. Built at a cost of £750m, Grosvenor Developments were behind the scheme to transform the heart of Liverpool. Employing 27 different firms of architects with master-planning by BDP. This view shows South John Street which is now a partially covered shopping and restaurant complex on three levels.

THIS PAGE:
The zigzag staircase links Paradise Street to the upper levels of South John Street and onwards to Chevasse Park. Combining both escalators and the staircase, this exciting design is enhanced by the lighting.

Chavasse Park. Part of the Liverpool One project,
this park with its wide expanse of grass and sloping
walkways has fast become a place of relaxation and a
meeting place. The Reverend Francis James Chavasse
was appointed Bishop of Liverpool in 1900 and
masterminded the plans to build Liverpool Cathedral.
His son, Noel served with distinction in World War I,
being the only soldier to win two Victoria Crosses.

Peters Lane Arcade, again part of the Liverpool One project. Designed by Dixon Jones Architects, this arcade uses a clever design of roof to give natural, even illumination, even on dull days. Note the cut-out in the architecture to give a view of The Bluecoat cupola. An important design consideration to much of the Liverpool One development was that existing iconic views should be preserved.

The Liverpool One Bridewell on Campbell St (Campbell Sq) of 1861 was once the lock-up and offices for the local police force. Today you may dine discretely at tables set in the old cells.

The Hard Day's Night Hotel and Mathew St. Hard Day's Night Hotel was opened in 2008 and is a Beatles-themed, luxury hotel. The building was formerly called Central Buildings and was designated as the backup location for the Allied Command Headquarters in the city, during the Battle of the Atlantic. Later it was used as offices on the upper floors and also housed the famous De Coubertins sports bar immediately prior to its closure and conversion. The building dates back to 1884 and was designed by Thomas C Clarke.

The Philharmonic Hall. The home of the Liverpool
Philharmonic Orchestra, this building was designed
by Herbert J Rowse after the original building was
destroyed by fire in 1933 and rebuilt soon after.
Depending upon your point of view, the plain-styled,
brick-built exterior, is ugly or sophisticated. The interior,
however, has a wonderful accoustic space and the
image here shows the daunting view a nervous soloist
would face as they came up on stage. Incised Art Deco
female figures, representing musical moods, adorn the
walls of the auditorium.

Across the road from the Philharmonic Hall is the Philharmonic Hotel, of 1898–1900. The brewer, Robert Cain, felt that the drinking public should be exposed to the enlightenment of quality architecture and the interior is ornately decorated in marble, mahogany and glass. This even extends to the famous gentlemen's toilet and users of the facility have always to be prepared for the invasion of camera-toting tourist parties!

ABOVE:
The Hilton Hotel, part of the Liverpool One development.

RIGHT:
Ben Johnson's magnificent airbrush rendering of the City of Liverpool. Exhibited now at the Museum of Liverpool. This 244x488cm acrylic on canvas was started in 2005 and completed in 2008 with the help of 11 assistants.

This view from *Matou Pan Asian* restaurant terrace towards the Museum of Liverpool and the Mann Island development. The canal link leads towards the Albert Dock basin.

The great liners abandoned Liverpool in favour of Southampton almost a century ago. With the completion of a deep water landing stage at Prince's Dock they have returned, marking the re-emergence of Liverpool as a tourist destination.

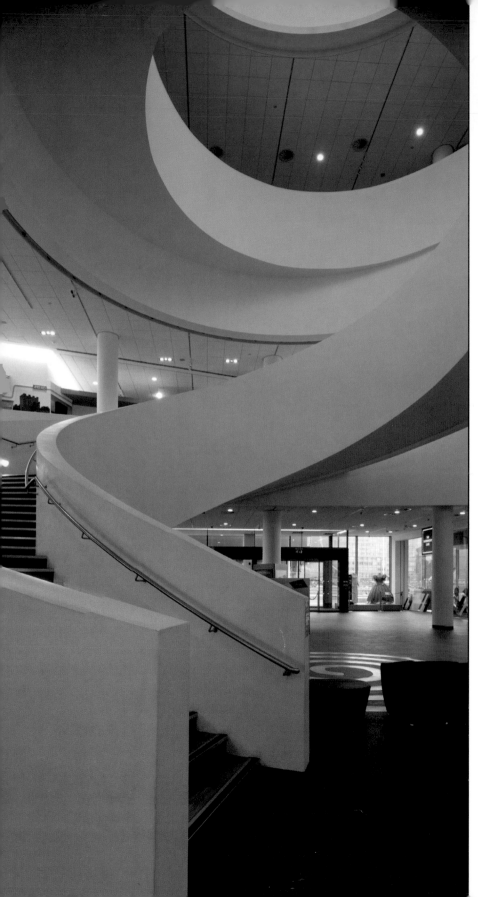

The Museum of Liverpool. Officially opened on the 19th July 2011.

Western Approaches Museum.
The Western Approaches Command HQ was responsible for control of the Western Approaches during WW II, the main sea route from the Americas to Great Britain. It was relocated from Plymouth to Liverpool in 1941. Situated in the basement of Derby House, part of Exchange Buildings, it was known locally as the *citadel* or *fortress* due to the extensive reinforced concrete protection.
The museum is open from 1st March to October each year.

CHAPTER 5

THE DOCKLANDS

The docks were the financial boiler house that powered the rise of the city from an obscure hamlet/port (one ship registered in 1609) to the largest single system of enclosed docks in the world. The peak of the docks' pomp was marked by the construction of the Port of Liverpool building in 1903–07. Prior to that, Liverpool had grown rich, partly on a triangular (and ill-gotten) trade of slaves, sugar and cotton. The dock infrastructure was needed to service fleets of sailing vessels unloading across more than 26 docks and 200 acres. By 1740 Liverpool was the largest slave-trading port in Europe. Changes began with the arrival of ever-larger iron-hulled ships and the abolition of slavery itself had a limited effect on the prosperity of the port. Iron ships, no longer limited by the size of trees soon outgrew the docks and slowly drifted away, the great liners to Southampton (from 1907), the other vessels to Manchester (via the newly opened ship canal), and the other ports of the UK.

The legacy of this great wealth lies in the massive structures of these enclosed docks and their adjoining warehousing. The need to provide secure, bonded warehousing to comply with the 1803 Warehousing Act ensured that the docks were enclosed behind literally miles of high walls, up to 18 feet in height.

Other massive structures included the Grain Warehouse (designed by GF Lyster in 1866 – 1888), built by the Mersey Docks and Harbour Board who shrewdly noted that the repeal of the Corn Laws would open the way to trade with North America. Of equal bulk was the Tobacco Warehouse built between 1897 and 1901.

Today, with the Royal Seaforth Docks now trading only in containerised vessels, 95% of dock jobs have vanished and the massive, older infrastructures have become residential areas and tourist playgrounds, only occasionally returning to their former usage as props and backgrounds for period drama filming. However, the great liners have returned more recently, with the completion of the new landing stage built out into the river itself, an engineering feat the Liverpool dock-building forefathers could not (or would not?), manage.

The tug *Svitzer Bidston* pulls the tall ship *Dar Mlodziezy* from the Sandon half-tide dock on route to the Mersey, in preparation for the Parade of Sail. The largest ships for this event were moored at this dock and the Wellington Dock prior to the parade on the 21st July 2008.

ABOVE:
Canal narrow boats waiting to go through the Stanley Dock lock system on the Leeds–Liverpool Canal. The Stanley Dock tobacco warehouse can be seen beyond the railway bridge.

RIGHT:
Stanley Dock tobacco warehouse is said to be the largest brick built building in the world, a total of 27 million bricks were used in construction. Fireproof in construction, it has been closed since 1980. Each floor is only 2.2m high, supposedly making it unsuitable for conversion to residential or office use. Built in 1901 it is a Grade II listed building. There have been numerous plans to redevelop the site and the building but these are yet to come to fruition. In November 2011 new plans were put forward and approved for turning the complex into apartments, shops and an hotel. Perhaps in the next revised edition of the book there will have been some progress!

RIGHT:
The Stanley Dock Warehouse is now used for the weekend heritage market and has also found favour with TV and film production companies for period drama.

BELOW LEFT:
The drinking fountain is one of a number which were installed in the mid 19th century, commonly called a 'Melly' fountain, after the philanthropist Charles P Melly. Though most of his fountains were made from red, Aberdeen granite, this example is cast iron. It is situated on Regent Road at Nelson Dock. It is one of 33 sanctioned in 1859 by the Mersey Docks and Harbour Board in a futile attempt to keep the dockers out of the local public houses!

LEFT:
The Regent Road bascule lifting bridge (built in the 1930s and now renovated) brings the main road across the waterway between the Stanley and Collingwood Docks. It is from this point that you can view the Victoria Tower (see page 128) looking towards the river across Collingwood Dock and looking in the opposite direction into Stanley Dock is the entrance to the Leeds-Liverpool Canal lock system. The main picture shows the recently refurbished lock system, which brings narrow boats down from the Leeds-Liverpool Canal to the dock system through a flight of four.

> "…All ham but tells of the commercial pride of the decades…"

LEFT:
The Victoria Tower, situated at the dock gates into the Mersey was built between 1847 and 1848 and designed by Jesse Hartley. It was described by Pevsner as 'All ham but tells of the commercial pride of the decades.' The tower's bell provided tidal and weather warnings to shipping. The pidgeons in the inset picture give scale.

RIGHT:
At the far end of the dock system, to the north, stands the Royal Seaforth Docks. This modern, fully containerised port handles more cargo than the port of Liverpool ever handled in days gone by. The 'mountains' of scrap iron on the quayside are exported all over the world and provide substantial business for the port.

The most northern part of the dock system is the Royal
Seaforth Dock. Here an Atlantic Carrier of the ACL
line can be unloaded, reloaded and returned into the
Mersey within the space of twelve hours. The MDHB
operation operates 24 hours per day, every day except
for the three Bank Holidays at Christmas and New Year.
It is the speed of turnaround which results in few sailors
spending time (or money) in the surrounding areas of
the docks, which once thrived on this sort of business.

In the distance can be seen one of the Belfast ferries
heading into the port.

Great Howard Street runs parallel with the northern docks and heading back into the city. The ultra-modern Beetham Tower and West Tower contrast sharply with the rear of the Stanley Dock Tobacco Warehouse, architecturally just over 100 years apart, but in reality, a totally different world. This view is taken just north from the point where the Leeds-Liverpool Canal joins the Stanley Dock.

CHAPTER 6

The Albert Dock

The climax of dock building for the Port of Liverpool came in 1846 when Prince Albert opened the new complex named after him and after the expenditure of £721,756. The dock and the surrounding buildings addressed the need to provide a secure berth in a river with a large tidal range, as well as compliance with the 1803 Warehousing Act. This act permitted importers of taxed goods to defer payment of the excise duties (provided the goods were securely stored and supervised) until they were moved to their place of sale – as today, it was all about cash flow. This security requirement influenced the architectural design of the docks complex with its high walls, policemen's lodges and controlled gates. Goods travelled only a matter of yards from the ship's hold to their warehouse floor. In addition, the value of the cargo placed a requirement for a fireproof environment so as to reduce the costs of insurance. Devastating fires at both Liverpool and Hamburg in 1842 had highlighted the fire problem once again, and a number of full scale mock-ups of the Albert Dock buildings were tested to destruction before the architect Jesse Hartley was happy with his designs. It was the close proximity of the warehouse elevations to the water's edge which later prevented any modifications to the complex and this accelerated the eventual demise of the Albert Dock.

The arrival of ever-larger iron ships, no longer constrained by the strength and length of timber meant that the Albert Dock soon became too small and by 1914 hardly any ships actually unloaded there, although the warehouses continued in profit until the 1950s, storing tobacco, wines and spirits. They finally closed in 1972 and the images on pages 136–141 show the forlorn and dilapidated state they had fallen into by 1978. After a number of false starts and some threats of demolition, the complex was eventually saved, restoration starting in earnest in 1983. The refurbished buildings now hold museums (including the Beatles Story), an art gallery (Tate Liverpool), dwelling apartments, commercial offices and shops. The complex is the UK's most popular heritage attraction and has most recently been linked up with the new Liverpool One development which is just the other side of the Dock Road and provides a conduit into the city centre. The area sometimes reverts to its past, as a bustling seaport, when period dramas are filmed and the walkways are filled with costume-clad extras and sailing schooners are once again moored dockside.

The Albert Dock complex is laid out in five separate warehouse stacks, each five storeys high, but none having the same floor plan. They are: The Colonnades (where Tate Liverpool is situated); Edward Pavilion; Atlantic Pavilion; Britannia Pavilion and Warehouse D (which houses the Maritime Museum).

PREVIOUS PAGES:
Views of the Albert Dock circa 1978. Top left is a view from the building which is now home to the Liverpool Maritime Museum. It is possible to see the crane on the quayside of the Edward Pavilion (still there, but refurbished) and also the World War II bomb damage on the Atlantic Pavilion building, which was not repaired until the restoration started in the mid-1980s.

On the right-hand page a view of the Colonnades Pavilion which are now luxury apartments.

THIS PAGE:
Engraved markings in roman numerals on the dock wall alongside the dock gate indicate the water level within the dock. Such matters were of concern to the dock workers as they tended the mooring ropes.

OPOSITE PAGE:
TOP RIGHT:
Where the Maritime Museum is now situated, the indent facing the Pier Head used to be enclosed by a wooden framework. The metal chute is still in existence though it has been moved against the inner wall of the building. The discarded tools of the trade are poignant reminders of the once thriving dock.

LEFT:
Jesse Hartley was keen to employ the latest technology for off-loading ships and manoeuvring them about the dock. The Port of Liverpool had some of the first cranes after Hartley saw them in Newcastle. Although the availability of cheap labour slowed their adoption, they were eventually replaced by the newer electrical powered systems. This example is by Wm Wadsworth of Bolton.

THIS PAGE:
The exterior wall within the courtyard of what is now the Holiday Inn in the Britannia Pavilion. The hoist is still there though the hut has long been taken away.

The Last Word

It is only eight years since the first book in the series, *A Portrait of Liverpool*, was published in 2004. The Paradise Project (Liverpool One) was due to break ground in November 2004 after many years of planning, which can be traced back as far as 1958, though, in reality, serious plans to redevelop around Chevasse Park and Paradise Street were put forward in 1999. The Mann Island Development, Museum of Liverpool, the Pier Head redevelopment and Lime Street Gateway were still in planning stages. Yet by 2009 the first edition of *Liverpool The Great City* was able to focus on the finished project, with the other schemes well underway. Now, in June 2012, all are complete, open to the public and are worthy of the world-wide recognition they are generating. It will be interesting to see what the next eight years will bring. I suspect that the majority of the regeneration around the Pier Head is now complete, with only the Princes Dock area to be looked at, and focus will now move towards the Northern Docks and Peel Group's plans for its Liverpool Waters project which aims to redevelop 60 hectares of disused northern dockland, adjacent to the Stanley Dock.

Technical

For those interested in such things.
I use a variety of equipment:
Nikon D3s and D3x cameras with 14–24mm, 24–70mm, 70–200mm, 500mm, 24mm PC lenses and also a Walker XL 5x4 field camera.

Acknowledgements

With grateful thanks to all companies and individuals who have helped with the making of this book and who gave access to interesting vantage points. Clients have commissioned some images and we thank them for allowing their use within the book.

We have drawn extensively upon the great scholarship of Joseph Sharples, John Belchem, and Quentin Hughes to guide us around the city and its history, we thank them all.

PMcM MMcN

National Museums Liverpool, Matou Pan Asian Restaurant, Liverpool One Bridewell, Neil McKenzie of Epson UK, Duncan Cooper of Calumet Photographic, Liverpool Cathedral, Liverpool One, RIBA NW, ISG Construction, DAKSA Seaforth Cornmill, Grosvenor Estates, Liverpool Civic Trust, Liverpool Hard Days Night Hotel, Castlewood Property Management, Cunard Buildings, Mason Owen Property Consultants, Holiday Inn Hotel, The Victoria Gallery and Museum, Mersey Travel, The Western Approaches, Glenn Howells Architects

Rob McLoughlin, John McDonald, Alaster Burman, Charles Brooks, Derek Gainford-Jones, Mike Walker, Ben Johnson